The Tinder Principle

the Never-Ending Quest for Love/Sex

The Tinder Principle

🍀 the Never-Ending Quest for 🍓 Love/Sex 🔥

Chapters

Introduction

Why I Did It?

I remember the night my entire Life changed: I went from 1-2 matches per day, to the entire World liking me overnight.

How did I do it? *By being myself and.. uploading the <u>right</u> picture.*

=~=~=

Originally, this book was written for males, in order to help them become more successful on Tinder.

=~=~=

I'm now going to teach you how to become a Tinder Expert, by sharing my knowledge and experiences with you..

Enjoy

<u>Pre-Requisites</u>

Before Entering

- Be good.

- Be clean.

- Look neat.

- Don't be a complete junky.

- Expect the unexpected.

- Try not living at home.

- Be affluent (preferably rich and famous).

- Do sports.

- Have cool hobbies.

- Be a vegan or vegetarian.

- Be secure.

- Be without fear.

- Be honest.

- Be positive, be charming.

First Session

Establishing the Profile

What makes a profile great?

A great profile stands out from the rest —
it's the one that is *different*.

If you do it right, your profile will
obliterate her entire deck and make her
forget all her other matches, in-the-blink-of-
an-eye.

=-=-=

Create a profile that tells a story.

Something that captivates the minds of
the viewers, and spurs on their imagination
(for the better): Be a hero, not a villain.

=-=-=

Don't upload an existing picture — create
something new and unique for the occasion,

but never say you did it *just* for Tinder, because then you'll be viewed as *needy*, and this you want to avoid at all costs.

=~=~=

Selfies are frowned upon by Tinderellas (even though they themselves upload them all the time).

Nonetheless, if you've got an attractive visage and a genuine smile, a good selfie will land you plenty of matches.

=~=~=

No animals or children should be featured on your profile, nor landscape shots or group pictures (once there's a more attractive person on your profile than yourself—you've already lost).

=~=~=

Tinder is about presenting your best version of your Self to the World—so make it count!

=~=~=

No 'silly' faces or 'too strained' faces—a relaxed face emits a calm demeanor, which is a virtuous attribute, and a sign for a composed spirit and an upright personality.

=~=~=

No sunglasses! Eyes are extremely important and need to be visible at all times.

Whether a person is honest or not, can be quickly discerned by taking a glance into their eyes.

=~=~=

If you decide to cover your head, make sure you're not trying to hide any balding spots, because that's the first thought that'll come to their minds.

=~=~=

If you wanna show off your muscles— don't! Out of principle they'll left-swipe.

=~=~=

No gym pictures—unless it's like the coolest gym picture ever!

SECOND SESSION

Attracting Matches

What to do once you've matched?

Should you write first or wait?

Tinderellas expect you to write first, so you may either choose to wait or make the first move.

Don't keep 'em waiting for too long, because, out of spite, they'll keep you waiting *forever*.

In other words: Write them within the first 60 seconds of matching—or make it the first 5 minutes of matching, but anything beyond that is pushing your luck.

=-=-=

The best opener I've thus far found is this:

"hey.. "

Why?

Because she'll usually respond immediately, and is already slightly aroused by the time she does.

=~=~=

Use any tools at your disposal to heighten the mood (smileys, GYPHS, Tinder-Reactions, voice-messages).

=~=~=

Don't ever send dick-pics, unless she wants you to.

=~=~=

If a Tinderella writes first it means one of the following three things:

#1 You're her very first match...*ever*.

#2 She really likes your looks.

#3 She's totally unattractive.

=~=~=

Don't sign your sentences with a question-mark (even when asking a question) or exclamation mark, for that matter.

=-=-=

Avoid the following words: Please, thank you, may I, Sex, Fuck, No.

=-=-=

Don't ever insult a Tinderella (even though she might just be playing you)— remain calm and focus on another.

=-=-=

Through words alone you've got the opportunity to build rapport between you and your match—therefore: Choose your words carefully.

=-=-=

These are the 3 most commonly asked questions on Tinder - I also like to call them:

<u>The 3 Deadliest Questions On Tinder</u>

..and how to answer them best:

#1 Where are you from?

-Earth.

#2 What do you do?

-Live.

#3 What are you looking for?

-Found!

=~=~=

A Tinderella will most likely respond with "You don't even know me." When you answer the latter question with 'Found!'

There's no easy way around this, but at some point you're going to have to stick your neck out a little and actually start fighting for this person's time (just do it in a suave way).

Meaning: You want to get to know her, but in person. Tell her this in a sweet way, but don't suck-up too much. Keep your responses laconic; never ask twice; and if she doesn't respond immediately — start chatting with another.

=-=-=

Rule of thumb is: Always keep her waiting for half the time she keeps you waiting, e.g.: If she keeps you waiting for 8 minutes, keep her waiting for 4 minutes.

=-=-=

Anyone who fails to respond in a timely manner is usually not worth your time — don't invest anymore of your time and energy into pursuing this person...if she doesn't respond at least once within 24 hours — forget her.

If she doesn't take the time for you — stop giving her yours.

Third Session
Setting Up the First Date

- Be succinct, be direct.

- Let your emotions flow.

- Let your openers be great and unique ('Are you like a famous person' try it, because people love hearing others talk positively about them).

- Don't write 1.5x more than she does (but this rule may be bent).

- Around the 6th message ask her out, by suggesting something she might like to do (you'll need to learn to become an expert at quickly cold-reading people).

- Get her to constantly respond in the affirmative (meaning: Her answers should be 'Yes' to everything you say).

- Chatting for up to 2 hours a piece will get her to stop viewing you as a stranger, and may even get you to meet her right away, if you do it right. Remember: Words are your best weapon. Use them to turn her on.. but do it slowly. Women are all about a slow build-up.

- If you feel you gotta wait, then chat with others or do something else — never wait for a Tinderella to respond!

- Be nice, but not too nice, otherwise they'll waltz all over you.

- Don't be overly patient, otherwise she might think you don't care or are too afraid — timing is everything!

- Suggesting to meet at yours or hers too early on might get you unmatched or put into the Silent-Zone. But usually she'll say something like, 'Let's meet outside first.' Do it — you just landed your first date.

- Every now and then you'll come across a Tinderella, who, once you've sufficiently turned her on with your wit and charm, will agree to meet you at hers or yours (right away) — these are the best matches. Treat them well, and they'll become your 'Fuck buddies'.

- Don't be pushy after she says no; although applying small amounts of pressure can get her to change her mind — but it's a risky gamble, because she might just end up unmatching you.

- Never threaten a Tinderella into giving you what you want — the real trick lies in getting her to offer you the things you want. Remember: Tinder, as well as mastering Life, is all about your internal psychology — project positiveness, and good things shall come your way. Just don't be a push-over. Stand your ground! But don't be overly aggressive about it —

be playful and tease her, and keep the conversation fresh.

- Don't be clingy.

- Don't let on that she might be your only match you're currently chatting with, or only match, for that matter—keep cool and continue chatting with the others (if there are others). If there aren't: Then don't respond immediately, unless you're both totally engaged into each other's conversations.

- Get to know her as much as humanly possible, in as little time as possible.

- Be observant, pay attention, remember the finer details of what she says.

- Don't ask her stuff such as, 'What's your favorite color,' or any type of ultra mundane questions—ask these casually when you're walking together side-by-side.

- The secret to any woman's heart is getting her to naturally like you — sounds paradoxical: *"getting* her to *naturally* like you,"* but that's essentially it.

- It's all a big data-transfer. Don't upload your information onto her too quickly — take your time, otherwise she'll feel overwhelmed.

- Overwhelming her may be good, but only if you're planning on actually staying together with her for a very long time...that is: If you've got the means of providing sufficiently, speeding things up may be advantageous.

FOURTH SESSION

Meeting Your Match

- The first Date needs to be memorable and unique.

- Choose exotic locations (if you didn't manage to directly meet up at hers or yours)—good girls, who are considering entering into a relationship with you, will most likely kiss on the first date and sleep with you on the second one.

- Dress comfortably.

- Parks are better than watching movies together (going to the cinema)—you want to be able to talk to her, and not let some outside force entertain her,.. but *You*!

- *You* *are* her Entertainment—make it the performance of a lifetime.

- Be inventive, be creative.

- Avoid overly crowded venues, such as bars, restaurants or discotecks...also remember not to let your money do all the talking for you — it's all about you two, not what your money can buy!

- Kiss sooner than later (sometimes even directly when meeting her for the very first time)...I've kissed a lot of them on first site — and it felt absolutely great, because we had already built up a connection via words, etc., beforehand.

- Try moving it back to hers after you've kissed, but don't mention it more than once — if she hints at your remark again, casually say, 'sure, why not' (don't be overly excited about this, because it's just another one of her tests to see how you'll react). If she changes her mind, no worries — there'll be others. Learn letting go (if need be), or just waiting a few more days, but don't quit Tinder (yet...wait!).

- Always take your time but make sure you, ultimately, always have it your way. Remember: You're a leader, and she's joining *your* team...the *winning* team!

- If she declined your initial advances, sporadically keep trying (by holding her hand or putting your arm around her). Eventually she'll kiss you. Or she'll leave. But a woman who's still sticking around after the 3rd try is bound to kiss you on the 4th swing. Or she'll just leave. No biggie. Next!

FIFTH SESSION

Post-Coitus

- If she doesn't write you again, there's hardly a chance of ever meeting her a second time around (just how it works)—but write her at least one courtesy-'had fun with you'.

- Make plans with others immediately.

- Don't expect this Tinderella to become your steady girlfriend, after just one time of sleeping with her. Therefore: No need to apply unnecessary pressure.

- Don't focus all your thoughts and attention on what just happened—remain calm and enjoy your accomplishment, before moving on to the next.

- If she's really interested she'll let you know.

- If you really like her, but she doesn't like you back the same way — focus on another. Never tell a Tinderella you like her, unless she says it first.

- Most Tinderellas will say stuff like, "I'll immediately delete the app now." — just a bunch of BS.

- They'll go back on Tinder after having slept with you — this is called micro-cheating…I've not met a single one who's ever stopped tindering after having slept with me, even though some turned out to be my girlfriend for a few months thereafter.

- Nonetheless, don't expect to land a saint on Tinder — just continue tindering around after having bedded her — there's no shame in it, she's doing the same.

PITFALLS

- Don't chat for too long, a date should be planned within the first 24 hours of matching.

- Some people are in open-relationships— avoid these, unless you're into that sorta thing.

- Some girls will specifically target you for favors—avoid these as well!

- If you use profanity too soon, you might get reported. Profanity, if used at the right moments will work in your favor. Always wait for the right moment, by slowly building towards it.

- Some Tinderellas will want you to join her and her friends for drinks or whatever— do it, or decline and tell her to text you her address afterwards. If you wait long enough and keep remaining steadfast she might actually do it—chances are good.

- Don't mention the threesome until you've slept with her (this can be right after having slept with her)—she'll most likely say yes, if not, no worries.

- Some Tinderellas will immediately decline you when meeting you for the very first time, and send you back home—politely leave. Never make a scene. Suggest to go out for a drink somewhere and enjoy one last friendly chat—if she still says no, say goodbye.

How To Get 1000 Matches in Under a Week

If you did everything right when creating your profile picture, you'll be able to match with everyone/anyone.

Upgrade to Tinder+(Plus, or Tinder Gold); right-swipe on everything without looking; change locations overnight (whilst sleeping)—preferably to a country (or place) where it's around 8 PM.

When you wake up, quickly garner the new matches of the location you charged overnight, and then just switch back to your current location (or another where it's again around 8 PM—best time to Tinder, btw), and just continue swiping until there's no one left to swipe on.

Repeat this for up to 3 days straight.

On the 5th day you should hit the 1k mark.

PS: Don't swipe for more than 3 hours a piece—unless you want your eyeballs to explode.

PSS: Whilst swiping, occasionally look away from the screen and just glance at it every-now-and-then—to make sure you haven't accidentally clicked on and opened a profile.

There are also ways of having a computer program do this for you—but this is how you do it manually.

<u>Miscellaneous/Additional things to consider</u>

<u>How to get her to give you her number?</u>

Build rapport and ask to switch to Whatsapp. If she's reluctant, tell her it's to hear her voice — if she still doesn't go for it — try meeting her, and don't ask for her number anymore.

If you've already given her your number, yet continue writing each other on Tinder, without her having added you (or messaged you on Whatsapp), nor given you her's in return — it's best to just wait and still try to meet her outside first.

But at this point I'd say you've not built enough rapport (a meaningful connection) with her. And you might've just landed your very first strike (X) with her.. this is bad.

If you keep the conversation interesting enough, she'll eventually ask, or tell you, to give her your number—it's all about that initial connection you build off of your gambit (and the next 20 sentences that follow).

Don't ever give a Tinderella your number too soon—she'll just think you do this with every woman on here.

If you give her your number too soon, and she doesn't give her yours—be careful now because you might end up never meeting her (nor getting hers).

If a Tinderella writes you the following sentences, it means you might've already lost her (stop writing so much):

"too soon"

"too quick"

"too fast"

<u>How to get her to invite you to meet?</u>

Once a positive connection has been established between the two of you—she'll eventually suggest meeting on her own, usually by first asking you this question (or a variation thereof): 'What are you doing now?'

Respond by suggesting to meet up. If she says she's busy, don't respond anymore—more-often-than-not a Tinderella who declines your offer, will talk herself into it again, *if* you don't respond until the offer you're looking for is in.

Just be patient and watch her go from 'No, I'm busy tonight (meeting with friends, bla bla bla)' to 'You still wanna meet?'

If you feel like there's a somewhat meaningful connection between the two of you—offer to meet her before she offers it (but never ask more than once—for anything, even in real life... and never dwell or become bitter over anything—she'll end up having to prove herself to you again).

<u>How to get her to want to fuck you?</u>

If you haven't already slept together, once you've built a positive connection through sweet & exciting words—you can mind-fuck each other, by writing each other more of these arousing words, until you finally meet.

Once your words turn her on, meeting her is just a stone's throw away.

If you can get a girl wet with words alone, and/or voice-messages (before ever having met or slept together, etc.), then she most definitely can't wait to meet you, and is purposefully building the hype, in order to - when you meet - fuck your brains out!

Even if you're not as attractive as on your pictures, part of her will still like you, and might even make an exception.

WORDS NEED TO EXCITE!!!

<u>How to get her to keep wanting more?</u>

Never overdo it (although some might like the pressure), nor do too little!

Keep things exciting and fresh.

Once you both like each other—you'll be at the back of her mind (constantly—and she'll be fantasizing about sleeping with you in her spare time).

The greater this bond between you gets, the more time you'll end-up spending together: She'll start inviting you to almost anything she does (and she'll expect you do the same).

Once you've reached this point in your relationship—it's time to start experimenting with each other in bed: try new things together (but always be careful!).

Reaching this point can be as soon as the 10th day, or within the 3rd week.

After this you may consider her your official girlfriend—congratulations.

<u>Outro / Conclusion</u>

Trust is the Holy Grail of Espionage—once broken it's like crumbled paper—never-ever the same (nor smooth) again.

Relationships are built upon trust—if you break or tarnish that very basic foundation—how can you expect things to flourish between the two of you?!

Once your basic foundation has been corrupted, your relationship will be of a sad & stressful nature—essentially not a healthy, nor a conducive relationship.

Once you broke the Trust—she'll always be afraid of you—and will tell herself that you're <u>*not*</u> the One.

Trying to desperately repair/mend said trust will lead to nowhere—let go and learn not to break the trust!

Many people believe that true Love tolerates *EVERYTHING*—NOT TRUE!

True Love only accepts True Love as a worthy companion.

Don't expect love by acting like a total douche.

Only by being genuinely good may you experience true Love—everything else is a complete farce.

THE HIDDEN CHAPTERS

80%-90% of all males *only* right-swipe. With females it's the exact opposite.

Most Tinderellas go on Tinder because they're looking for a serious relationship.

Once you land her, she'll probably delete the app, but not her account.

Shadow-Stepping / Resetting

Delete your entire account. Then create another one with the exact same phone number, etc. (I even recommend using the same pictures you used on the previous one — maybe even play around a bit with your name, age, as well as your description text).

Log back in, and you'll automatically be transplanted back into the TOP 100 — if you do this a few times in a row, anyone who's currently swiping will continuously see you

re-appearing in the rotation, become
suspicious and eventually right-swipe you,
and ask you how you do this.

Tell her it's top secret. Never yield to her
demands—if she's curious, let her be.

Sometimes you might not get any
matches, just repeat the process until you
do.

Word-of-caution here: To them you'll
seem like the *rogue* one—some might even
mistake you for a bot ... therefore:

Be. Careful. When. Shadow-stepping.

=-=-=

DO. NOT. REPORT!!!

Just left-swipe on any nuisances—Tinder
isn't really about the swiping and what may
come next—it's about chatting with and
meeting your match(es).

Report only if you're 100% sure that the user is a bot. Otherwise just left-swipe or unmatch again.

=~=~=

If people are mean, usually they'll just get unmatched again, or placed into the infamous SILENT ZONE.

=~=~=

You've just gotten *"silenced"* — this means she'll not talk to you anymore — she might've even muted you. Unmatch this one immediately (or just wait until you shadow-step again).

=~=~=

Dear males, there are two things you absolutely need to learn:

#1) Never physically nor psychologically abuse a female (or any person for that matter)..

E V E R ! ! !

#2) Do not stalk or insult a female. If you're an aggressive person, I suggest becoming sweet and soft — for even softness may deliver a blow!

In a nutshell: Never frighten a female. Appreciate her and enjoy getting to know her.

=˜=˜=

Don't tinder if you're about to leave or go on vacation. Tinder when you get there.

=˜=˜=

Tinder Gold is good for sniping individual matches.

=˜=˜=

Super likes don't raise your chances, may even diminish them.

=˜=˜=

For best results set your age and location bars to max.

=~=~=

The more Love you invest, the better the Sex gets.

THE END

PS: Guys, stop wearing dark socks with shorts..

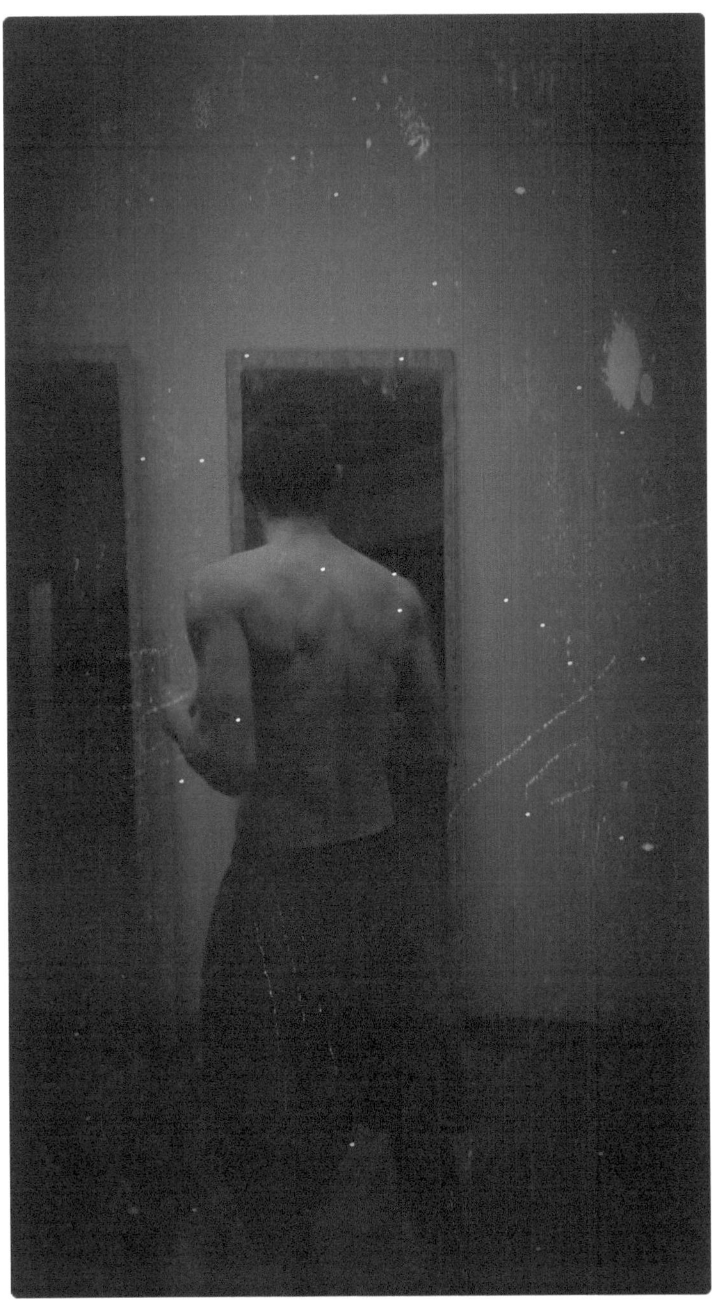